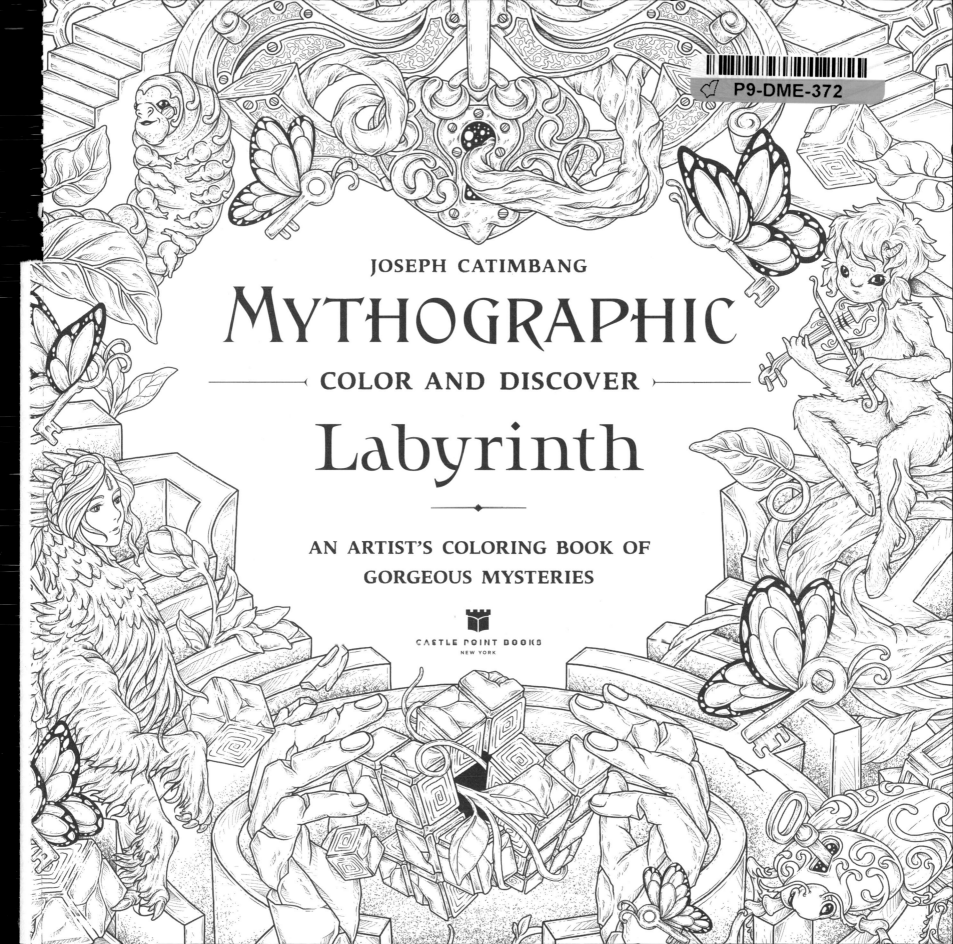

JOSEPH CATIMBANG

MYTHOGRAPHIC

COLOR AND DISCOVER

Labyrinth

AN ARTIST'S COLORING BOOK OF GORGEOUS MYSTERIES

CASTLE POINT BOOKS
NEW YORK

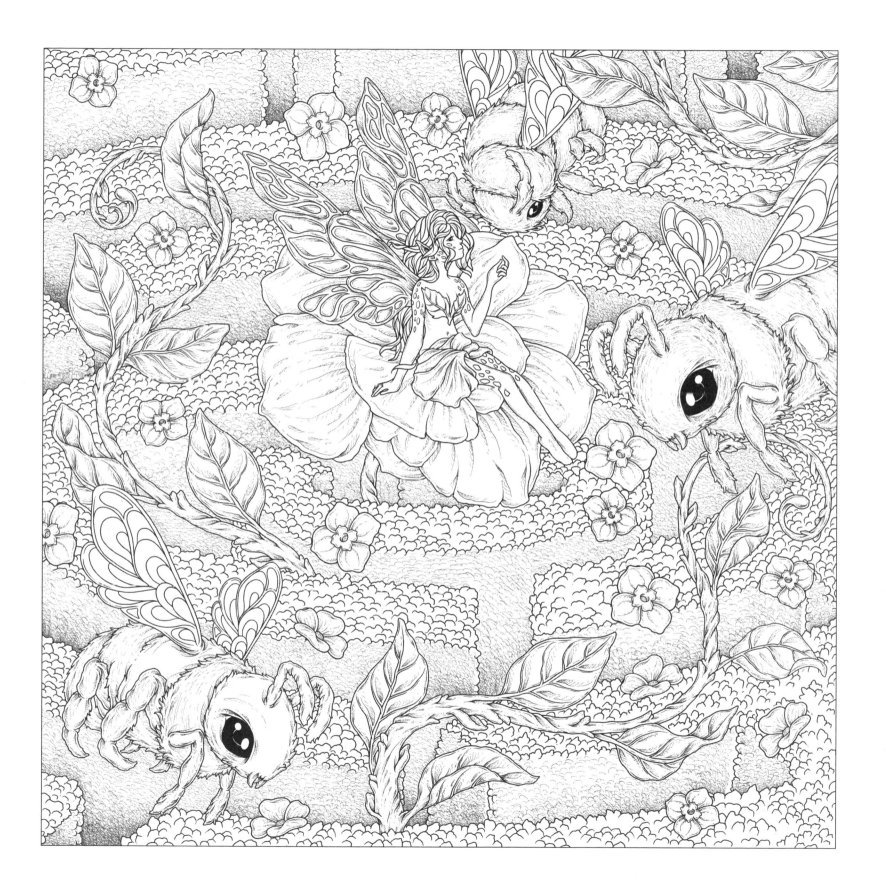

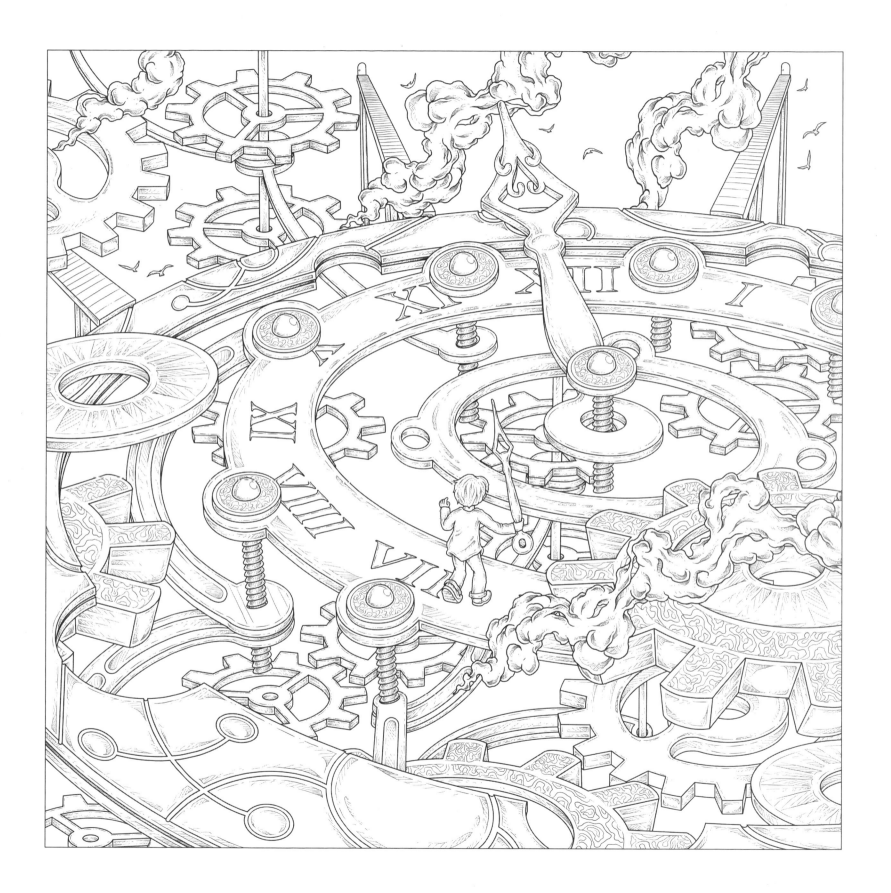

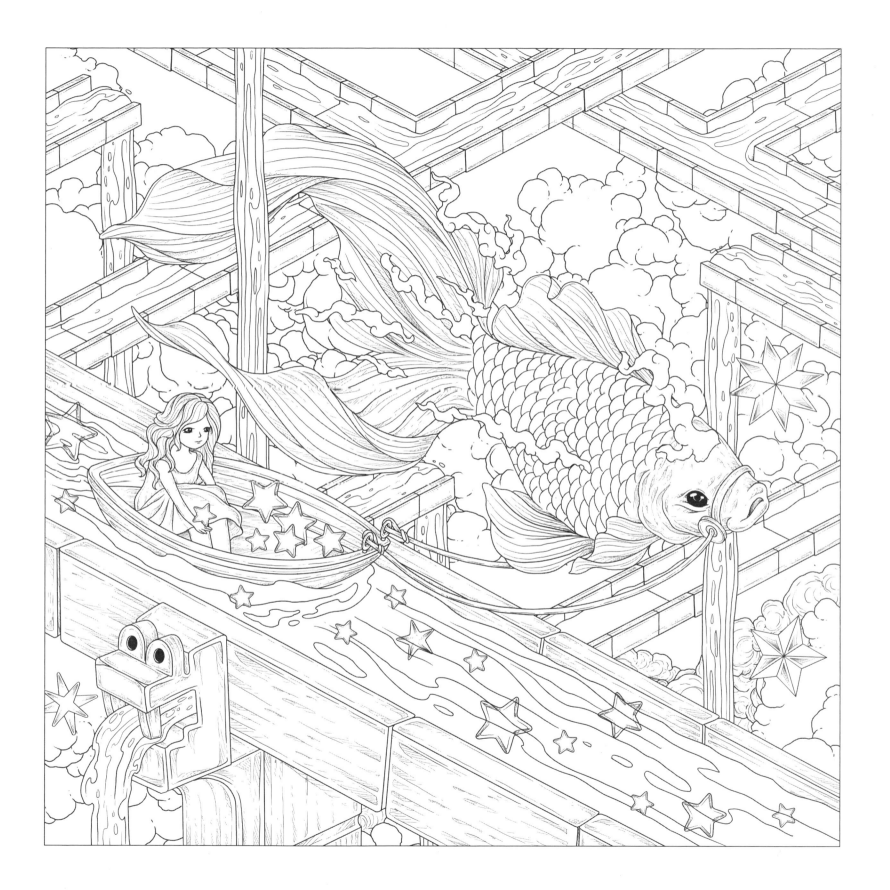

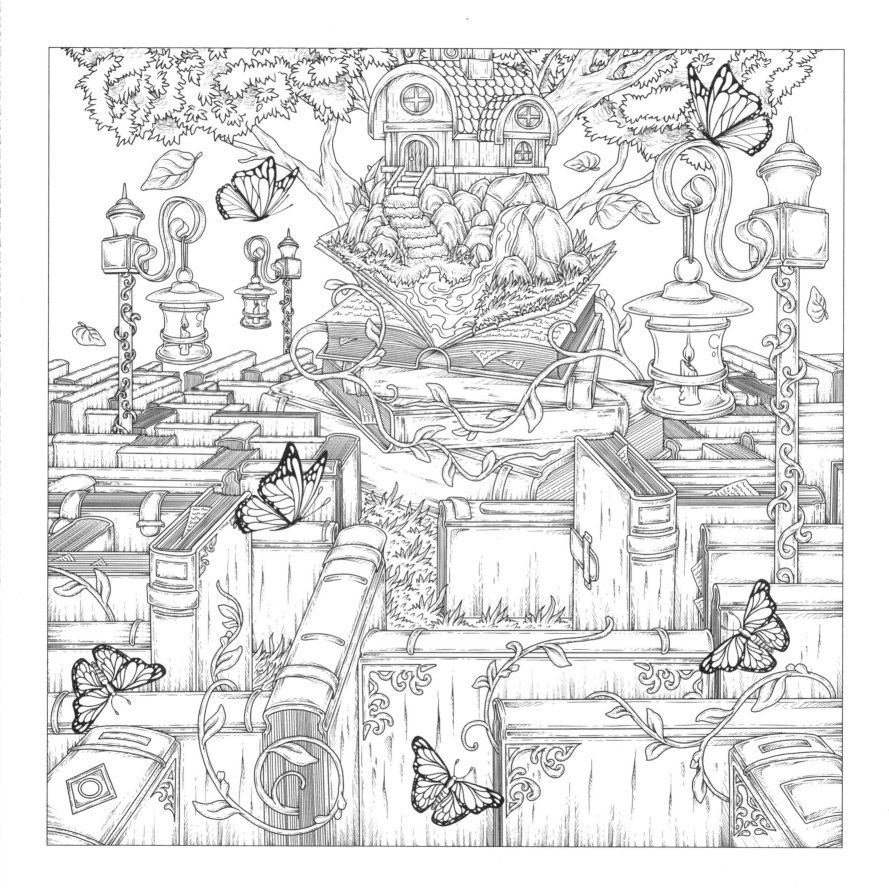

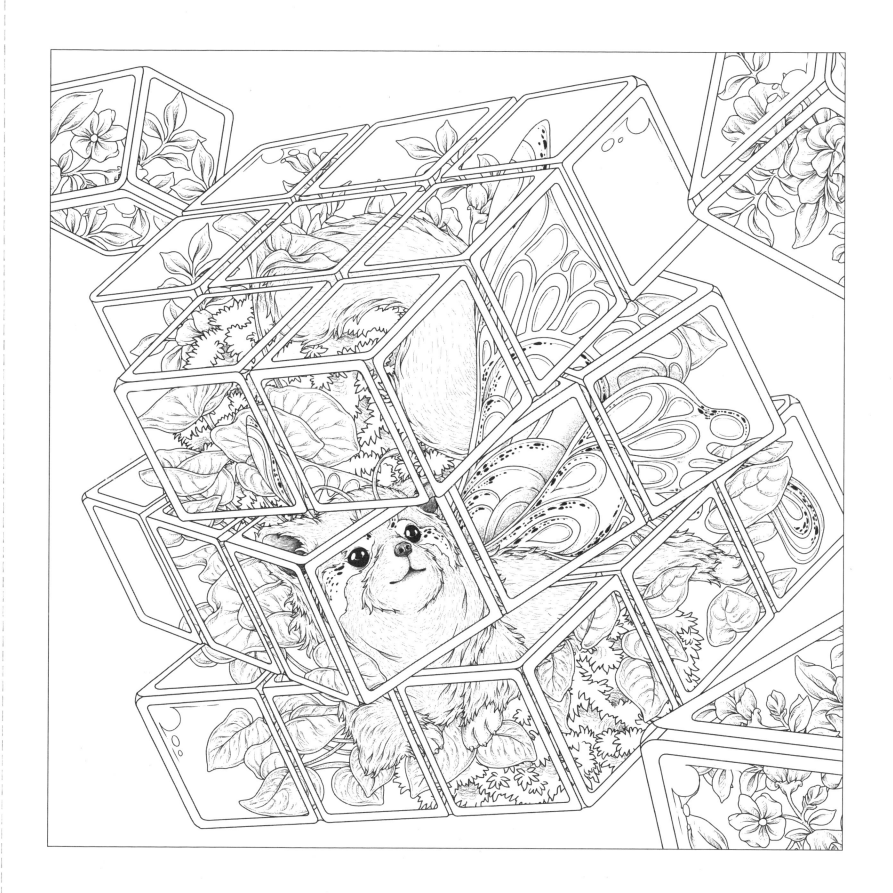

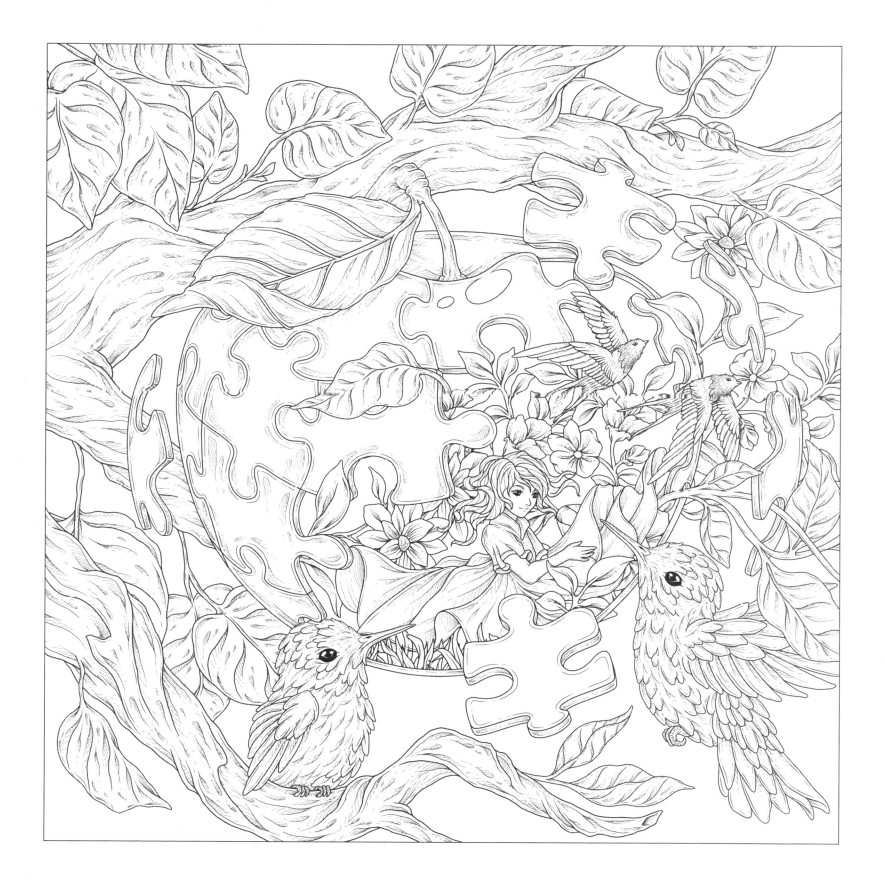

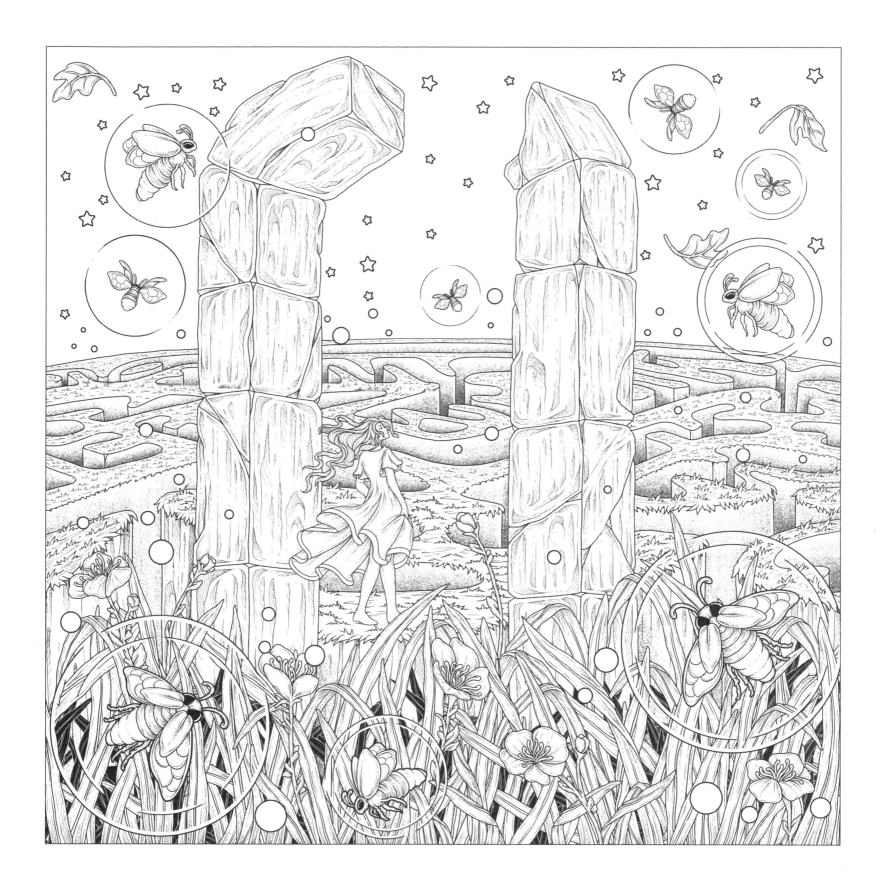

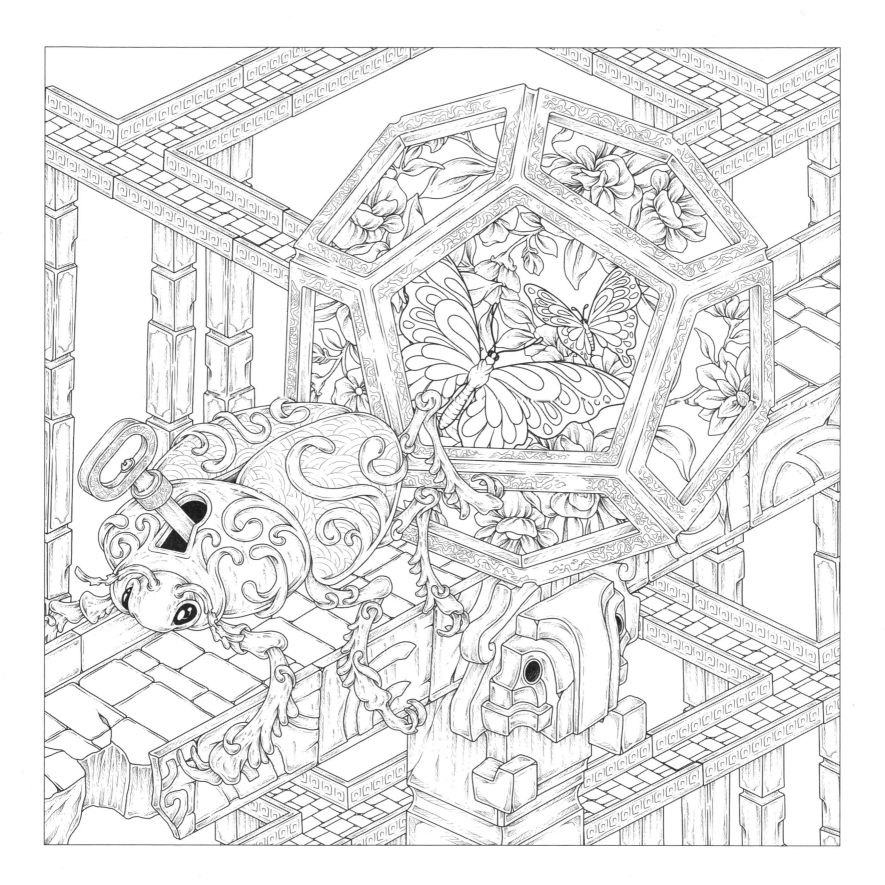

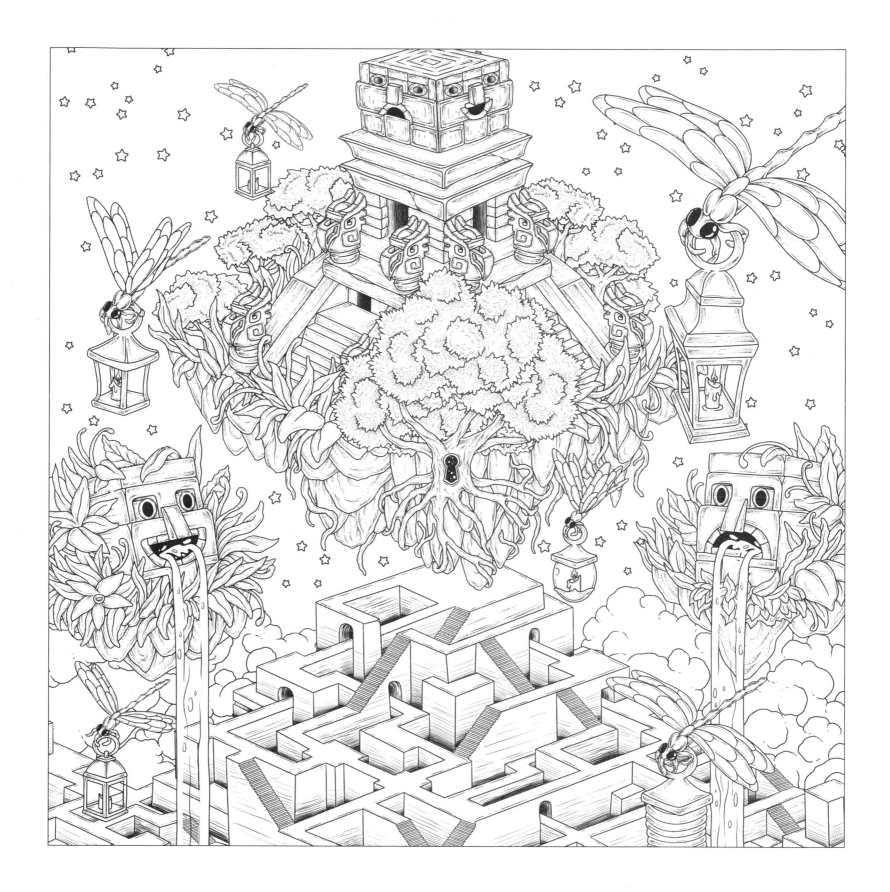

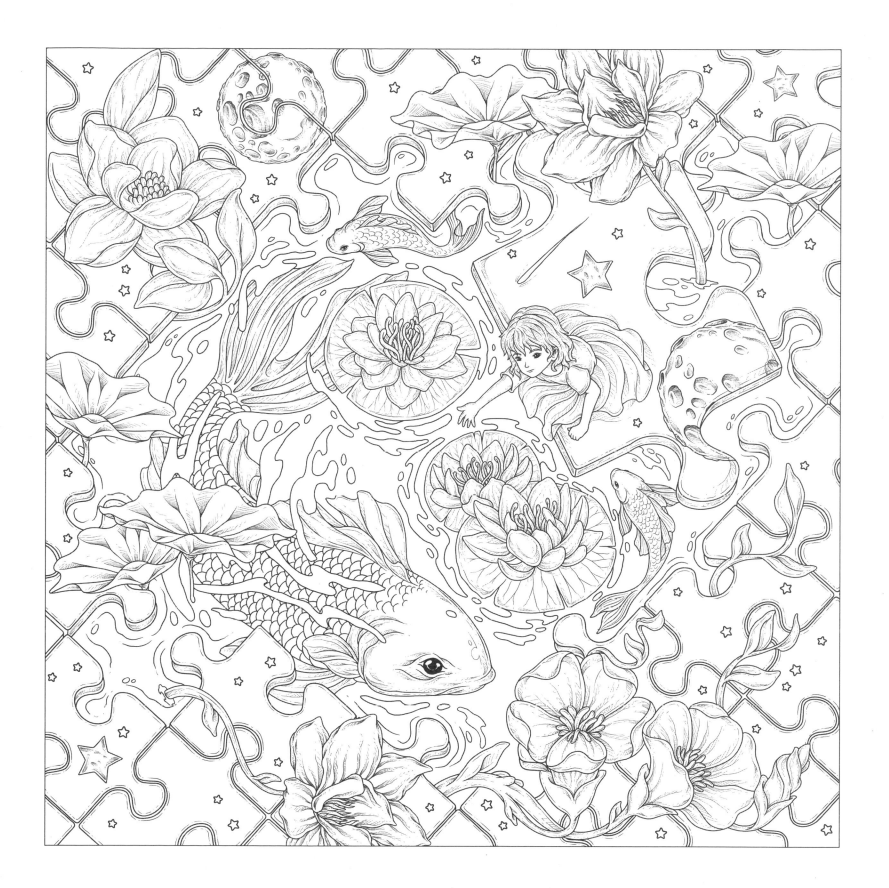

Discover more of Mythographic

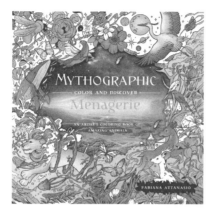
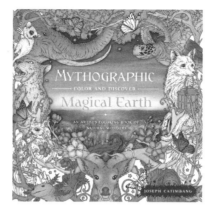
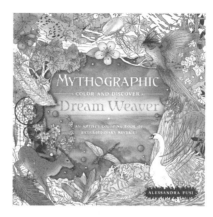
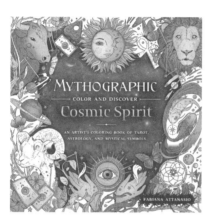
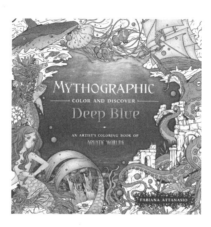

ISBN 978-1-250-28781-6 (trade paperback)

Cover design by Young Lim
Edited by Monica Sweeney

Our books may be purchased in bulk for promotional, educational, or business use.
Please contact your local bookseller or the Macmillan Corporate
and Premium Sales Department at 1-800-221-7945, extension 5442,
or by email at MacmillanSpecialMarkets@macmillan.com.

First Edition: 2023

10 9 8 7 6 5 4 3 2 1